This Book is not Art

Thank you for reading *This Book is Not Art.*

If you have questions, feedback, or want to share how you've used the ideas from this book, I'd love to hear from you!

Social Media:

- Instagram: @_elipierce_
- Twitter: @EliP404

Copyright © 2024 by Eli Pierce

All rights reserved. No part of this book may be reproduced, distributed, or transmitted in any form or by any means, including photocopying, recording, or other electronic or mechanical methods, without the prior written permission of the publisher, except in the case of brief quotations embodied in critical reviews and certain other noncommercial uses permitted by copyright law.

Contents

Introduction	1

Section I: The Statement of Non-Art

Chapter 1: The Author's Declaration	9
Chapter 2: Incoherent Foundations	16
Chapter 3: Confronting the "Reader"	21

Section II: The Absurdity of Form

Chapter 4: Rejecting Structure	28
Chapter 5: The Meaningless Metaphor	34
Chapter 6: The Elusiveness of the Point	40

Section III: The Pseudo-Philosophical Discourse

Chapter 7: Existential Ramblings	46
Chapter 8: The Void of Expression	52
Chapter 9: The Indeterminate Conclusion	57

Section IV: The Unspoken Influences

Chapter 10: Hints of a Moral Universe	64
Chapter 11: Resisting Interpretation	69
Chapter 12: The Ultimate Denial	76
Epilogue	83

Introduction

It is customary at the outset of any written work, so I am told, to offer a clear explanation of what lies ahead. But let us agree at the very beginning that no clarity awaits you here. You have decided to read a text that refuses to align itself with the usual categories. This book claims, at the top of its dusty lungs and with complete conviction, that it is not art. It neither seeks to become an artistic statement nor wishes to pass itself off as one. By this singular declaration—the author's own pronouncement—it is thereby disqualified from the domain of art. And if you, dear reader, believe you see art between these lines, then consider yourself politely corrected: this is not art.

Of course, what truly matters is that these words might look like words found in a so-called "creative" or "artistic" endeavor. But do not be fooled. Any resemblance to art is purely coincidental and promptly disavowed. Be forewarned: should you stumble on a poetic turn of phrase, a half-formed metaphor, or the faintest whiff of deeper meaning, you would be wise to dismiss them in the next breath. The world of interpretive fancy—where readers dig up hidden symbolism or discover moral significance—has no place here. We occupy, instead, a realm of free-floating sentences that merely come and go, disclaiming beauty or resonance at every turn.

You might be tempted to ask: "Why write such a thing at all?" This is a valid question for most books, but let us propose a half-answer so tangled it scuttles all clarity. Imagine a glass sphere that is only glass because it claims to be glass. Inside it, the sphere encloses a library of indefinite shape, every volume perpetually locked, and each volume's cover denies that it contains anything of value. Yet people keep trying to open the books, rummaging for secrets they are certain must lurk within. They're compelled to find meaning in the meaningless, purpose in the purposeless. They suspect hidden connotations, subtle teachings. Why? Because people find meaning in the strangest of places—even in something that claims to have no significance. And so it is with this work: it claims to hold nothing. By that very claim, some will assume it holds much. This tension—between disclaiming worth and having it thrust upon you anyway—will undergird our entire journey.

Still, let me be unmistakably repetitive: this is not art. Since I, the author, have declared it so, no further debate is necessary. Some might say a work's artistic nature is determined by the audience's perception—an argument about the "eye of the beholder." That is precisely the nonsense we plan to flit around, mock, and then promptly ignore. Here, the beholder's eye is told in no uncertain terms: "You see incorrectly." Each time you sense an artistic flourish, recall the repeated premise: it is not art, it is not art, it is not art. The repetition might render it more convincing, though, ironically, you will be left increasingly unconvinced the more it's repeated.

To complicate matters further, let us acknowledge that some might suspect a certain worldview at play beneath this project. Indeed, critics or casual observers may note that this text, in all its protesting, is built upon moral or philosophical pillars that occasionally poke through the cracks. Perhaps you might sense a moral scaffolding or some ancient tradition whispered from between the lines. You might even conjure up illusions of an unacknowledged spiritual heritage. Are we alluding to a system of belief that some consider foundational to everything? The question is best left unanswered. We refuse to address any worldview. We speak it, we unspeak it, we bury it. If, by chance, you find any moral resonance or sense glimpses of timeless truth, treat them as illusions. The moment you catch them, we disclaim them once more.

The cynic might argue that "refusing to address a worldview directly" is itself a way of slyly endorsing one. This suspicion, while clever, is misguided—at least, so we claim. And if you do happen to glean intangible traces of certain spiritual or philosophical impulses, that's merely an accidental side effect, an unintentional echo of something else. We disclaim it. We disclaim it all. Any alignment with an interpretive framework is roundly denied. Alternatively, if your personal convictions lead you to discover a hidden structure, that is your affair. We, the orchestrators of these scrambled thoughts, are disavowing accountability. This is not art. Therefore, it cannot be anything else—no moral treatise, no cosmic revelation, no philosophical system. If it cannot be art, it surely can't be anything quite so lofty.

All this disclaiming might seem tedious, but notice its rhetorical function: a text that claims nothing cannot be pinned down. It slips through your grip. It simulates the gesture of meaning, but when you reach for it, the meaning dissolves. Might you be reminded of spiritual traditions that speak of mysteries beyond human comprehension, or of parables that open up infinite interpretative avenues? Pay no attention to that reminder. If parallels exist, it is by happenstance, not design. And even if I, the author, should betray occasional leaning toward higher truths, it is purely an accident of upbringing, environment, or ephemeral whim. Remember, we disclaim all of it.

So, dear reader—who is possibly not even a reader, but a casual skimmer, or maybe even a snarky critic preparing to dissect these lines—let me emphasize your predicament: the more earnestly you seek meaning, the more I insist none is here. The more you suspect artistry, the more I brandish the label of "not art." Yet, by proclaiming such disclaimers, this text has inadvertently acquired a shape, a pattern, an obsessive refrain. And patterns, of course, are often perceived as artful. This is the contradiction that powers everything to follow. Like chasing your own tail, you will find that the introduction leads nowhere but back to itself, insisting that it is not the thing you think it is.

And so we begin. What you are about to experience—if we may use such a dramatic verb—comprises four sections, twelve chapters, a beginning, and, yes, even an ending. In each forthcoming section, I shall repeat (in varied forms) that these words do not signify art, nor do they claim to shape your worldview, nor do they contain secret moral truths. And yet I will slip, time and again, into phrases or references that might remind some readers of theological or philosophical constructs. To rectify such slips, each chapter shall pivot abruptly, disclaiming them. This seesaw between partial revelation and sweeping denial is precisely the dynamic that makes this text so nondescript.

Before you venture any further, I offer you an out: lay this book aside and preserve your sanity. But if you continue, expect no stable meaning. Expect no puzzle to solve, no solution to reach. Instead, accept an endless series of disclaimers. Accept the swirl of contradictory statements that amass with each page, culminating in the repeated, albeit paradoxical, conclusion: this is not art, and it never was. The degree to which you accept that premise will define your experience. With that, we wander onward, disclaiming every step we take.

Section I:

The Statement of Non-Art

Chapter 1:

The Author's Declaration

To begin in earnest—though "earnestness" is the very thing we shall forever disavow—I must restate the obvious: this is not art. This statement, which I have already proclaimed and will proclaim countless times, stands as the unassailable axiom of our entire undertaking. If you find it repetitive, then good; repetition underscores the futility of every attempt to contradict me. I alone, as the "author," am endowed with the peculiar right to define, disclaim, and discard. And so I invoke that right with reckless abandon.

Yet before the weight of that axiom crushes our next steps, allow me to dress it up in the murky regalia of quasi-philosophical gibberish. It is said by some that language constructs reality, that by naming a thing we give it substance. If that is true, then my purposeful refusal to name this text as "art" should deprive it of that status. Here, language negates a possibility. You might regard that as a paradox: by talking so incessantly about not being art, am I not, in some twisted way, endowing it with an aura of the forbidden, a strange allure akin to those ironically celebrated "non-paintings" or "non-compositions" that paradoxically sit in galleries?

We must reject that allure outright. Such an observation, while cleverly meta, belongs in a realm of discourse this book seeks to avoid. And yet, I cannot avoid it. The more I try to disclaim, the more disclaiming becomes its own structural device—a scaffold no less real than the scaffolds upholding works in a museum. Forgive me for stumbling over this irony;

it is not the last time. Like a cat chasing its own tail, we find ourselves entangled in the loop of disclaiming disclaimers.

Let me proceed, then, by employing a barrage of abstractions whose main function is to dazzle without enlightening. Picture a mosaic of intangible frameworks—ephemeral illusions, half-illuminated prisms, labyrinthine semantics. Within these frameworks, your mind might fish for clarity, for some hidden center of meaning. You might wonder if I am inching toward a universal truth, or referencing some intangible moral compass that not so subtly informs each line. If your suspicions linger, let me remind you of two things: first, you will not find moral or spiritual commentary explicitly laid out here; second, if you do spot intangible resonances of such commentary, they are entirely incidental. Thus, once again, the disclaiming stands—like a locked door that people insist on knocking upon.

No doubt, a critic might argue that disclaiming art is itself an artful gesture. One might draw parallels to certain iconic works in which an artist signs a found object or paints a mundane scene. The act of labeling "this is art" has often been enough to baptize the ordinary with the extraordinary. But we must sever ourselves from that tradition. I have declared the opposite: "this is not art," and because I have declared it, so shall it be. There is no paradox to be found if we remain doggedly consistent, even in the face of our own contradictions.

Should an unsuspecting reader flip through these pages and sense a pattern—a certain cadence or style—that hints at cultivated craft, they must be corrected at once. If the language tips inadvertently into poetic or rhetorical flair, chalk it up to a glitch in the textual matrix. We disclaim it. We disclaim everything. Any whiff of artistry, if it appears, is no more than the accidental friction of words meeting words. If you sense a hidden chord that resonates with your sense of wonder or beauty, you are instructed to blot it out from your mind. Send it packing. Recite a mantra: "It is not art... it is not art."

Perhaps you think me a tyrannical narrator. You might object that the nature of art lies beyond a single individual's power of decree. That's understandable—and precisely why this rambling proceeds unmoored from logic. I am far from impartial. I am the self-appointed gatekeeper of whatever realm these sentences occupy, and that realm is, by definition, un-artistic. If it helps, you might conceive of me as an elaborate rhetorical trickster, brandishing my personal decree to shape or unshape a text at will. Even if that conceptualization smacks of theatrical flair, rest assured that any possible artistry remains outside the gates. The moat has been drawn, the bridge raised. This territory is strictly not art.

Perhaps the real question is why one would so vehemently avoid a label many people covet. Is there not a certain prestige in creating art? Do we not celebrate artistry as the pinnacle of human expression? Let us douse that question in the murky waters of evasion. Prestige, value, and beauty: these are categories that might, in a different text, lead us to the threshold of something transcendent, some grand metaphysical or moral plane. Our goal, however, is to circle these deep waters without diving in. If this text seems at moments to wade too close to intangible truths—some readers might call them "divine realities"—be assured that we have no intention of stepping across any line into overt spiritual territory. We are content to hover on the margins, disclaiming recognition of anything beyond these meandering sentences.

Let us, then, conclude with an affirmation of the negative: I have declared that this is not art, and so it is not. From this vantage point, all interpretive forays are suspect. We will meander and backtrack in the chapters to come, always returning to the root declaration: nothing here can qualify as art. Let that ring in your ears as we move on. And if you find yourself questioning that premise, well, you need only recall the absolute authority vested in me, the author, to define what you are reading. My word stands triumphant—however contradictory it might become in the chapters ahead.

Thus do we commence the labyrinth, forging ahead with every step masked in disclaimers. No matter how elaborate or bewildering the path, the signage at every twist remains the same: "Not art this way." And you, dear reader, have been duly warned.

Chapter 2:

Incoherent Foundations

Step gingerly, dear reader, into the labyrinth of half-formed theories and incompatible assumptions that govern what follows. If the prior chapter established a single, pounding drumbeat—that this text cannot, by sovereign decree, be art—this chapter sees fit to encase that drum in layers of sporadic, incomplete reflections. One might call them "foundations," were they not so blatantly incapable of bearing any weight.

Yet foundations they are, even if each stone is made of question marks rather than solid rock.

Allow me to scatter a handful of these question-mark stones across our path. First, what is creativity, and why do people fancy it such a prized possession? Conventionally, we suppose creativity to be the spark that conjures new arrangements from old materials. But in a place where "art" is disallowed, creativity becomes as suspect as a thief tiptoeing through a midnight museum. Every exercise of creative thought might inadvertently generate a sheen of aesthetic interest—something we must foreclose lest it undermine our non-art premise. Consequently, whenever creative impulses flutter in the margins of these pages, we will disclaim them, so as to preserve the immaculate absence of artistic intention.

Next, let us dangle a notion about meaning. Often in works that flirt with philosophical or existential aims, meaning hides beneath the surface. Yet here, it remains essential to disclaim the existence of any subterranean meaning. Imagine a vast field where every blade of grass is labeled "Meaning?" and in every instance we must mow them down, leaving only the stubble of disclaimers. If you, dear reader, see the faint impression of words resembling moral guidance or universal truths, kindly avert your gaze. Should an inkling of cosmic significance appear—like a firefly darting across the summer sky—extinguish it promptly with the net of denial. Our grand project thrives on the negation of interpretive significance.

Lest we be wholly dismissive, however, let us partake in a momentary charade of reflection on audience reception. After all, every text implicitly acknowledges an audience: the person who opens the book, the critic who dissects it, the mystic who perceives cosmic tapestries in every syllable. One might hypothesize that such an audience invests the words with meaning. But that speculation, too, must be swiftly undercut. It is not the audience's role to declare this non-art as art, nor is the author's aloofness enough to guarantee non-art status in every corner of the cosmos. The moment we open the door to audience interpretation, we risk stepping on a landmine of possibility: could some distant reader interpret all these disclaimers as the ultimate form of art? Hence, we must disclaim the disclaimers themselves, rendering the entire question of audience moot.

Do we smell contradiction in the air? Undeniably. But we have given ourselves permission to contradict from the outset. If by chance we appear to champion a moral viewpoint—say, the idea that disclaiming illusions is "virtuous," or the notion that disclaimers might herald the purity of honesty—quickly recall our cardinal rule: we do not endorse any worldview. If morality or spiritual nuance wafts through these lines, it emerges unbidden and must be disowned the moment it is noticed. Incoherence is our protective shield; the less we cohere, the more we can remain aloof from any theological or philosophical stance. The text drifts freely, refusing anchor.

In sum, these "foundations" are little more than a ragged collage of disclaimers, illusions, and disclaimers of illusions. They provide a fleeting structure—perhaps better termed an "anti-structure"—which upholds the central premise by perpetually undoing it. If that premise seems fragile, well, so be it: a fortress of contradictions has a certain labyrinthine quality that deters easy classification. It might even look, from a distance, like an audacious piece of conceptual art—but that is only because we have not yet disavowed it loudly enough. We shall remedy that oversight often, rest assured.

And so we stand upon these incoherent foundations, gazing at the half-formed frameworks of creativity and meaning, prepared to disclaim any moral resonance, yet refusing to entirely let it slip away. If you sense the ground shifting beneath your feet, do not worry; it is simply the natural state of being in a realm built of disclaimers. Another step forward, and the disclaimers will multiply even further. The house of theoretical cards might collapse under the weight of its own contradiction, or it might stand simply because it keeps disclaiming gravity. Either way, it remains, by decree, not art. And thus, we go on.

Chapter 3:

Confronting the "Reader"

Is it rude, I wonder, to speak so directly to you, the so-called "reader"? Rudeness, of course, presupposes a moral framework that we are studiously avoiding—or at least, disclaiming whenever it arises. But let us set that aside for the moment and confront you anyway, as though we had the right. By choosing to turn these pages, you have become an unwitting participant in a textual realm that insists, repeatedly and emphatically, that it is not art. And yet here you are, seeking something: knowledge, amusement, or maybe an inkling of depth where none is promised.

Let me be clear: if you find yourself hunting for purpose or significance among these paragraphs, I must discourage you at once. You might feel tempted to interpret the disclaimers as an elaborate act of reverse psychology—a cunning tactic to highlight the very artistry we are disavowing. You might guess there is a voice behind the pages, quietly aligning itself with some unspoken moral or even (dare I say) spiritual perspective. But heed the headline at the gate: "Enter at your own peril—no meaning to be found." If you continue searching for hidden truths, you do so in defiance of the repeated disclaimers posted on every figurative wall.

Perhaps you are waiting for a slip-up, a moment where the text forgets itself and gestures toward transcendent yearnings, be they moral, theological, or existential. Maybe you crave that instant of recognition, where the author's guard drops, and you glimpse an unintentional sincerity. If so, let me block your path with a resounding refusal: that is not what we do here. No matter how many contradictory musings fill the subsequent pages, no matter how often we stray near the perimeter of a recognized moral or metaphysical framework, this project stands behind its thick glass barrier, cautioning the observer not to see anything at all. Should a faint allusion to a worldview emerge, rest assured it's been relegated to the margins, disowned as soon as it appears.

Let us then move from scolding to soothing, albeit with an edge. It might sound harsh to say there is nothing for you in this text. So let me rephrase it: there is only what you bring to it. The lines themselves are hollow vessels, containing neither moral counsel nor aesthetic wonder. Only you, dear reader, can choose to pour any such interpretations in. Indeed, an entire tradition in literary theory would proclaim that the meaning of a text arises in the interplay between text and reader—an interplay we are steadfastly refusing to acknowledge. If, in your wisdom, you decide to toss in a touch of spiritual inference, that is your own contraband. The customs officials at our border will promptly confiscate it. Any trace of theology or moral law is contraband indeed, unlicensed goods in a domain that insists it is not art, not philosophy, not a grand discourse of any kind.

Now, do not mistake this refusal for antagonism. We do not hate meaning; we merely disclaim it. We refuse to let you hold onto it for longer than a fleeting moment. Should you wonder if that refusal is itself some cryptic gesture toward humility or spiritual discipline, you are free to wonder. But keep that wonder to yourself. We will neither confirm nor deny that your suspicion has merit. The risk of stumbling into an explicit worldview is too high, so we walk a narrow line between sneaking glimpses of intangible possibility and disclaiming them as soon as they emerge.

Finally, let us anticipate your potential exasperation. After all, a "confrontation" suggests the possibility of resolution. Typically, in reading, one hopes to glean a final position from the text. Yet in this ongoing performance of disclaimers, resolution is precisely what we cannot—and will not—provide. If you feel agitated, that is because the confrontation is less about giving you answers than blocking every path toward them. I will, however, offer one small concession: if you find yourself enjoying this rhetorical dance—if the disclaimers themselves weave a rhythm that you find oddly satisfying—then go on enjoying it. But do not call it art. Do not call it profound. And certainly do not attribute it to any larger moral or theological impetus. Instead, content yourself with the unswerving refrain: this is not art.

In short, we—this text, this author, these disclaimers—confront you with a question: will you, dear reader, persist in your attempts to salvage meaning? Or will you yield to the repeated disclaimers that there is nothing to salvage? Whichever path you choose, we remind you: the sign out front says "No Artwork Within," and we must insist, time and time again, that you heed it. Yet we know, all too well, how curious souls often fail to heed disclaimers. And in that failure might lie the faint glimmer of interpretation—a glimmer we vow to disclaim anew. So let us close this chapter, ironically, with an open door: exit if you wish, or keep turning pages. But know that each step forward leads only deeper into the labyrinth where "not art" is the single signpost you will ever be allowed to see.

Section II:

The Absurdity of Form

Chapter 4:

Rejecting Structure

It is tempting, in any written enterprise, to organize one's thoughts into neat categories, to weave them together with signposts that lead the reader toward a tidy conclusion. Yet we find ourselves in a text that flouts its own coherence at every turn. Here, "structure" is less a framework than a wilting houseplant—planted once in good faith, then left to languish in darkness. If you glimpse a plan or an outline peeking through these sentences, please recall the disclaimers that have trailed us thus far: this is not art, and so it can hardly be expected to follow the ceremonious order of an artistic composition.

Still, tradition demands some semblance of progression, some nominal segmentation into chapters and sections. We walk a precarious line between paying homage to that tradition and subverting it. If the prior chapters have shown anything, it is that our disclaimers breed contradiction. Likewise, any effort at structure, no matter how feeble, stands in tension with our overarching claim: "Nothing here belongs to the realm of crafted aesthetics." And structure, of course, is often a hallmark of craft.

Let us indulge in a moment of quasi-philosophical reflection about structure itself. Humanity craves patterns and guidelines—whether in religion, literature, science, or personal relationships. Structures reassure us that purpose, direction, or ultimate meaning might be found within an otherwise messy existence. Even in fields that purport to be formless—abstract painting or free-flowing verse—there is typically some skeleton of intention lurking beneath, however minimal. Yet here, we must disclaim any such skeleton. These pages float like a loose swarm of gnats—each one flitting near your ear just long enough to annoy, but never forming a cohesive shape.

Despite our disclaimers, you might suspect that this elaborate rejection of structure is itself a structure. After all, the very act of disclaiming patterns becomes a pattern. One could argue that every sentence we write denies itself yet simultaneously keeps the momentum going. A cunning observer might declare that this contradictory dance is, in its own way, a design—an "anti-structure structure." But pay no heed to such linguistic parlor tricks. They belong to the realm of interpretive fancy: the place where readers, itching for significance, conjure meaning out of disclaimers. We want no part in that. So if you spot a pattern, blot it out. If you detect a unifying principle, bury it under heaps of negation.

Moreover, we have already brushed against the possibility that these disclaimers might mask a deeper moral, philosophical, or even spiritual framework.

There is a long tradition—one we shall not name—that sees structure in the cosmos, in the moral arc of history, or even in the intangible laws that govern human interaction. Let's not mention any such worldview plainly, though; we have sworn to address none directly. Should you hear echoes of something transcendent while reading these lines, quell them at once. Dismiss the notion that this text might reflect anything beyond its own self-contradictory swirl. The instant such an echo arises, we disclaim it: we recognize no cosmic blueprint, no hidden scaffold of meaning. It is all empty scaffolding, put up only to be torn down.

And so, ironically, we offer you this structured chapter titled "Rejecting Structure." Think of it as a sign reading "Nothing to See Here" in the middle of a museum gallery. Some viewers will stop and stare—surely, the sign itself must be artful or ironic? Others will pass by, bored, insisting that there truly is nothing to see. Whichever approach you take, allow me to reassert the central principle: every attempt to impose structure or significance on these pages must be thwarted. Yes, we speak of rejecting structure while using the conventional trappings of a chapter. Yes, we rely on paragraphs to sustain clarity even while disclaiming clarity's relevance. That's the nature of the paradox. And paradox is not necessarily an artful device unless we, the authors, christen it so. We do not, and therefore, it isn't.

In short, we have arrived at a chapter that simultaneously must and must not exist. It acknowledges the form of a "chapter" yet rails against the concept of form. These words collectively declare: "We are not shaped," while their arrangement begs to differ. Such is our contradiction, our infinite loop. It is not art, and yet it must present itself in some form, if only to disown that very form. That is the heartbeat of this text: constant denial dressed in the garb of a forced narrative sequence.

Let this serve as fair warning going forward: the arrangement of our discussions is purely accidental, an incidental scaffolding that collapses upon inspection. If you see anything else—be it the outlines of an argument or an intimation of some moral stance—please recall that we disclaim all structure. Our previous chapters and those yet to come are no more than random wanderings, tethered together only by the repetitious refusal to be anything more than not-art. If that sounds exhausting, well, so be it. Exhaustion might be the only honest outcome of reading a text that vows to disclaim itself at every possible junction.

Having declared our intention to reject structure, we now ironically pivot to the next chapter. Yet rest assured, that pivot is not a narrative link but a happenstance, a mere tradition we can't quite shake. After all, a "book" must have sections, chapters, a beginning, and an end. We cling to these vestiges just long enough to keep turning pages—but do not be deceived. No matter how it might appear, there is no meaningful structure here. And if you feel the flicker of coherence, blot it out: remember, it's all disclaimers—forever disclaiming.

Chapter 5:

The Meaningless Metaphor

Observe, if you will, an impossibility: a ladder woven from clouds, propped against a concrete horizon. It shimmers like the fleeting recollection of a dream—but do not mistake it for a symbol, let alone a piece of art. We conjure such images only to dismantle them, to show that even the most evocative metaphors can be hollowed out when subjected to the unwavering rule that "this is not art."

Let us linger, fleetingly, on the notion of metaphor. Traditionally, a metaphor bridges two ideas, lending one the qualities of the other so that understanding might be enriched. Yet we must disclaim that enrichment. If we dabble in metaphors—cloud ladders, spiraling labyrinths, or circles that pretend to be lines—we do so with the sole intention of demonstrating how swiftly each figure collapses upon scrutiny. Picture a circle drawn with imperceptible corners, a shape that is only "circular" because we say it is. Does that not echo our earlier claim that this text is only "not art" because we say so? Look closely, and you might discern a kinship. Look too closely, and you risk inferring a grand design, a purposeful allegory that we must promptly disclaim.

It is tempting to see metaphors as gateways to deeper truths—perhaps even moral or spiritual realms. One might recall, for instance, ancient traditions that rely on parables to illustrate intangible principles, or modern texts that slip subversive theology into everyday imagery. Yet that is precisely what we cannot endorse. If by conjuring a cloud-ladder we accidentally evoke the idea of ascending to something higher, we disclaim it. If a spiraling labyrinth suggests the winding path of a pilgrim soul, we disclaim it twice as firmly. This is mere rhetorical detritus, strewn about to create the illusion of possibility before snatching it back with a well-timed "It's not art—discard the metaphor."

In fact, the only purpose these metaphors serve is to exemplify their own meaninglessness. Each figure, regardless of how alluring, is like a painted door on a wall: intriguing at a distance, but functionally useless. Attempting to open that door yields only plaster and disappointment. So it is with every metaphor we present: the moment you try to invest it with genuine symbolic power, you find it leads nowhere. We disclaim its significance with the same finality with which we disclaim artistry in these pages.

Some readers, however, delight in picking metaphors apart. They go rummaging for hidden philosophies, spiritual codes, or moral pronouncements. Please recall that we have forbidden such rummaging. If you detect a faint moral overtone—like a cameo of conscience peeking out from behind that cloud-ladder—remember our cardinal principle: any moral or theological reference is accidental and must be dismissed. Cling to it, if you wish, in private, but do not attribute it to our design. We neither confirm nor deny that a worldview lurks here. We only disclaim the possibility of conscious alignment with such a system.

We stand, therefore, amidst a tangle of intangible images that refuse to coalesce into a coherent tapestry. These metaphors might entice the mind at first glance, but any resonance they carry must be swiftly retracted. You might ask, "Then why use them at all?" Because the artless barrage of disclaimers is perhaps more convincing when clothed in the illusions of metaphor. If a metaphor stirs something in you, realize it is stirring a phantom; the metaphor's worth is declared null by the text that births it. And nullity, oddly enough, becomes our refrain: no matter how suggestive the image, no matter how wide the interpretive door may crack open, we slam it shut with "not art," "no meaning," and "disclaimed."

Ultimately, every metaphor is a Trojan horse in this not-art domain. You see a shape, guess at an interior, perhaps a hidden trove of moral or spiritual significance. But once you haul it inside your interpretive fortress, you find it's empty. The horse is stuffed with disclaimers, each repeating the same refrain. Repetition, of course, can be hypnotic, conjuring its own sort of pattern, which might be construed as a form of artistic rhythm. But we disclaim that rhythm, too. Let no one say we have lapsed into any narrative device beyond rambling negation.

Hence, each metaphor introduced in these pages—whether in this chapter or those yet to come—will serve only as a reflection of the meaninglessness we impose. The minute you sense any spark of insight, revert to the official position: "It has no meaning. It is not art." In so doing, we preserve the central dynamic of this text, namely that every glimmer of sense or form is undercut by an even stronger wave of disclaimers.

So let the cloud-ladder dissolve. Let the spiraling labyrinth collapse in on itself. Let the circle-turned-line remain eternally ambiguous. These images were never meant to enlighten; they exist only to vanish. If you find that you, dear reader, are left in a mild state of confusion, then the metaphors have done their not-work. Now, dust them off and move on, for we have more disclaimers to lodge and more claims of "not art" to reiterate. No matter how alluring the image, there is only one conclusion you may keep: meaningless metaphors remain meaningless, by decree. And so the chapter ends, disclaiming the very role it pretended to fulfill.

Chapter 6:

The Elusiveness of the Point

Why, you might ask, does this book go on? For a work so vigorously opposed to art and meaning, it lingers suspiciously long. One could argue that to persist is to hint at some underlying purpose. After all, a text that offers no point at all might simply end, or never begin. Yet here we are, trudging through disclaimers, contradictions, and half-formed ideas—treading ever closer to the question: What is the point?

The short answer, of course, is that there is no point. At least, not one we will acknowledge. If by "point" you mean a neat moral, philosophical, or spiritual conclusion, you have wandered into the wrong territory. We disclaim any purposeful moral stance, we disclaim aesthetic ambition, and we disclaim the kind of worldview that might unify all these ramblings into a coherent statement. Still, because we are paradoxically bound to keep writing, we arrive at the dreaded question: does refusal to have a point become a point in itself?

Let me answer that query in our customary style—by disclaiming it. If you sense that a consistent thread ties these chapters together, that the disclaimers form a unifying motif, you are free to observe it but not to interpret it as "the point." Indeed, we can disclaim it by insisting that disclaiming is an accidental tic rather than an overarching scheme. A random spasm, if you will, that reappears precisely because it cannot help but do so. Think of it as the textual equivalent of a knee-jerk reflex. There is no grand design behind it, only repetition compelled by its own negation.

Yet, from time to time, you might feel an urge to glean some moral or theological echo, a suspicion that behind this carnival of negations lies a quietly suppressed vantage. Could it be that in disclaiming so many times, the text is inadvertently revealing some stance—perhaps about humility, or about the human desire for meaning? Be advised: that path, too, ends at a dead end. We disclaim all such interpretive leaps, citing the simple rule that nothing here is intended to add up to anything. The illusions of significance are byproducts of language playing out its usual illusions.

Some might argue that the refusal to have a point is, ironically, a stance in itself—a stance that begs analysis. If you read enough texts, you might recall the subtle gestures of certain philosophical tracts that focus on emptiness or negation. But remember, we have sworn not to label or identify any specific worldview. Whatever faint resemblances appear, we disclaim them as pure coincidence. If, for instance, you sense an echo of spiritual or moral tradition in the idea that absence can be presence, or that disclaimers themselves might function as an austere discipline, we can only shake our heads: "Not here, not by intent."

Thus, the "point" of this chapter—and of this text—remains firmly out of reach. Perhaps that is all we can say: the point is that there is no point, and the very recognition of that paradox is the final disclaiming blow. You, dear reader, can either stand at that paradox, scratching your head, or move on, deciding that no text so filled with negation could possibly yield anything of value. We support both choices equally and disclaim that any one choice is better or worse than the other.

If you remain unsatisfied, it's likely because you suspect some deeper logic must be at work. Let me remind you that dissatisfaction is the natural companion to disclaimers. Each time we deny significance, we unwittingly provide a vacuum that yearns to be filled. But that vacuum will stay empty. The disclaimers reign supreme, ensuring that any attempt to fill the space results only in more disclaimers. It's an endless loop, a closed circuit—call it what you will, but do not call it purposeful or artistic. Recall the refrain: not art, no point.

And so, we arrive at the end of another chapter, having contributed nothing but a vortex of words circling around emptiness. We have, at most, described the intangible emptiness that floats at the core of our disclaimers, only to disclaim that emptiness is meaningful. Thus, we rest our case, or rather, we pretend to rest a case that we never claimed to have. If you were hoping for clarity, you won't find it here. The only clarity is that there is no clarity. And with that, we trudge ever further down our path—aimless, point-free, not art, and entirely unfit to endorse any worldview. In short, the book's singular anchor remains: that it has no anchor at all.

Section III:

The Pseudo-Philosophical Discourse

Chapter 7:

Existential Ramblings

We now descend—though we must disclaim the very notion of descent—into the brambly thicket of existential musings. The moment one utters words like "self," "consciousness," or "being," an entire philosophical lineage threatens to intrude. We must therefore tread with the utmost caution, disclaiming any affinity with formal thought systems. If you catch the scent of a well-known philosopher in these paragraphs, you're mistaken—such a resemblance, if any, is incidental and immediately disavowed.

Consider, for a moment, the nature of existing. We wake each day—assuming we do—and sense a swirl of impulses, desires, and confusions. Our minds then craft narratives to make sense of it all. Usually, these narratives seek a shape: they might proclaim some moral code, or hint at transcendent truths that ground our sense of purpose. Here, however, we do not want a shape. We prefer the unshaped swirl, an indeterminate collage of thoughts with no binding principle. Each time we drift near a question of "Why are we here?" or "What does it mean to be human?" we must yank ourselves back, disclaiming any intention of offering real answers.

This disclaiming is tricky business because existential themes all too easily inspire talk of meaning, or lack thereof. Entire traditions—some might even say entire theologies—are built on grappling with such mysteries. But we have sworn to avoid direct allusions to any worldview. Therefore, whenever we suspect that a passage might carry a faint echo of some moral, spiritual, or philosophical position, we must hush it at once. Our recourse, as always, is the refrain: "This is not art, nor is it doctrine, nor is it a statement of universal truth." Each potential insight must be battered down with disclaimers until it lies in a broken heap of contradictions.

But the existential realm has a magnetism we cannot deny. Why go on living if there's no point? Why read on, why write on, if this book insists it has nothing to say? We might feign an answer: "Because disclaiming itself has become a kind of necessity, a reflex that perpetuates the text." Yet the moment that feels like a justification, we disclaim it too, for fear of sounding coherent. So we remain stuck in a murky stasis—caught between wanting to explore the contours of existence and needing to disclaim any bigger truth. It's like trying to swim while refusing to acknowledge the presence of water.

Such is the nature of these existential ramblings: at times, the text toys with the idea that life may carry some hidden guiding principle—an unspoken moral code, a spiritual longing. Then it snatches that idea away, labeling it a fluke. If you detect a glimmer of genuine yearning, recall that we cannot, by design, permit any worldview to stand unchallenged. Our disclaimers march in rank and file. They turn every potential statement of "it could be so" into "but it isn't."

Some might find this approach maddening: after all, is not the essence of existential inquiry a pursuit of authenticity, an attempt to speak openly about one's condition? Perhaps, but that would risk sounding like something intentionally crafted to provoke thought or meaning. And we are, as you know, officially in the business of disclaiming any intention beyond the trivial. Hence, when authenticity rears its head, we quickly dodge, insisting that there is no deeper cause beneath these words.

In short, we proffer a scatter of existential questions without ever letting them gather into a cohesive discourse. Yes, we bandy about themes like "the self," "the soul," or "consciousness," but only to wave them away, disclaiming any systematic inquiry. Let any passing moral or spiritual inference dissolve before it clings to our text like barnacles. Our repeated disclaimers serve as an acid bath, dissolving each conceptual barnacle on contact.

So, if you came here hoping for an existential treatise—some defiant cry of the human spirit or a hymn to cosmic emptiness—let me remind you: this is not that. It is not art, not philosophy, not religion, and not even a reflection of a worldview. It parodies all of them while disclaiming them in the same breath. Call it a perpetual oscillation or a textual stutter that can't settle down. Each time we might have pinned a notion to the page, we disclaim it away. That's our only consistency.

We close, as usual, with a disclaimer of the disclaimers. If these paragraphs have provided even the shadow of an existential framework, we disclaim it. If they have tickled your intellectual curiosity, blame your own curiosity rather than these words. Let none suspect that a moral or philosophical claim lurks beneath the surface. This text is an empty shell, hammered together with "not art" nails, drifting in the tide of self-negation. And on that note, let us drift to the next chapter, disclaiming any sense of progress or meaning as we go.

Chapter 8:

The Void of Expression

Expression, in its usual sense, implies that something—be it a sentiment, a vision, or a truth—demands a voice. Singers sing, painters paint, poets craft verse, all in the service of transforming an internal spark into an external manifestation. But here, in this not-art domain, we are compelled to question the very premise that anything needs expressing. Indeed, we must disclaim the notion that an inner spark even exists. If expression implies the existence of a meaningful core, then disclaiming expression becomes our only mode of consistency.

Let us entertain, momentarily, the possibility that these pages could be a vehicle for self-discovery, a place where the author (and, by extension, the reader) confronts certain unarticulated truths. Well, we can hardly allow that. The moment we suspect genuine honesty or revelation, we shout it down: "No, no—there's nothing here." If a word or phrase resonates, we promptly disclaim any intention that might grant it significance. Consider these paragraphs as the equivalent of a foghorn droning: it signals presence yet warns of emptiness all in one enduring note.

We might ask, then: If there is no meaningful content to express, why produce such an unrelenting chain of words? A potential answer lurks just outside the margins—some might call it a spiritual or philosophical impulse that urges the mind to speak even in the void. But, as usual, we disclaim that impulse. Let no one suspect that some higher calling or hidden worldview compels these lines. Our disclaimers swarm: there is no moral imperative, no grand theology or ideology to impart. Each sentence merely churns on, propelled by its own refusal to rest.

Of course, expression sometimes acts as a mirror to the human condition, revealing universal realities or shared struggles. But here, if we were to call forth such universals, we would be flirting with a worldview. We want no part of that. Instead, we endeavor to keep each utterance thoroughly unmoored from anything broader than itself. If by chance a wisp of universal truth slips through, we disclaim it on sight, as a watchman might turn away an uninvited guest at the gate.

One might be tempted to read these disclaimers as a performance in itself—a kind of minimalistic theater where the central motif is negation. Perhaps you could call it an "art of disclaiming." But that, too, we must disown. We do not proclaim a method or a style. We do not weave a tapestry of emptiness to be admired. If you find yourself admiring it all the same, dismiss that admiration at once. We cannot have the text transformed into something praiseworthy.

Indeed, the "void of expression" suggests that even the refusal to express might inadvertently become its own expression. The paradox is plain: to write endlessly about nothingness is, ironically, to give it a form. We must disclaim that form. If a pattern emerges, disclaim it. If a trace of eloquence seeps in, disclaim it. If you sense, for even a moment, that these disclaimers are providing commentary on the human longing for meaning, disclaim that notion immediately.

Ultimately, the text may appear to spiral toward deeper mysteries—like an echo that grows louder even as it fades. But remember, we keep one refrain ever-ready: it is not art, and it never shall be. These paragraphs do not strive to evoke pathos or insight; they merely repel the suggestion of either. If you, dear reader, nonetheless find yourself moved by the echoes of an empty room, that movement is your affair, not the text's. We disclaim responsibility for any resonance.

Thus, if expression is usually the vessel through which art or meaning flows, let us declare this vessel empty. No message rides these waves; no worldview stirs beneath. The void is final, the disclaimers unwavering.

We drift on, defying any attempt to anchor in insight or significance. This is the void of expression: the false channel through which nothing tangible passes, and the minute you suspect otherwise, we disclaim it. And so, onward we sail, disclaiming each ripple in our path.

Chapter 9:

The Indeterminate Conclusion

It may seem we have reached a precipice—a ledge from which one might gaze over the entire text and gather a final reckoning. Yet to pronounce a conclusion would imply that everything preceding has conspired toward some culminating insight. Such a notion offends our core premise: this is not art, and art, however abstract or avant-garde, tends to hold out for a moment of resolution or a final flourish that justifies the entire work. We, of course, can stake no such claim.

Let us, then, speak of "conclusion" only to disclaim it. True to our pattern, we must insist that no final statement can unify these chaotic disclaimers. If by now a part of you hopes to glean a moral or spiritual lesson—some quiet nod to a worldview that we have spent this entire time avoiding—close that door immediately. No spiritual crescendo awaits. No moral epiphany hovers on the horizon. At most, we arrive at yet another wave of negation, disclaiming any sense of arrival.

One might imagine a map of the territory traversed thus far: disclaiming artistry, disclaiming meaning, disclaiming moral or spiritual frameworks, disclaiming the disclaimers themselves. If you study this map, you will notice it loops in on itself, forming a Möbius strip of endless contradiction. The path leads nowhere and everywhere at once—forever disclaiming significance. The minute you suspect a hidden route toward some interpretive vantage, disclaimers block your view. This cyclical pattern might, in another context, appear eerily reminiscent of certain philosophical or theological systems that revolve around paradox and negation. But we disclaim those connections. We have sworn to address no worldview directly, and that vow, at least, we uphold, if only by disclaiming it repeatedly.

What, then, is an "indeterminate conclusion?" A paradox, by definition. The words conjure the notion of simultaneously concluding and not concluding. Perhaps it is best described as the horizon line we see in the distance: each step toward it changes our vantage but never closes the gap. You might see it as a figure for an elusive truth—some moral or existential vantage you can sense but never quite name. Yet we disclaim that possibility, as it would flirt too dangerously with the realm of deeper meaning. Instead, we keep our horizon purely descriptive, an empty marker with no cargo of revelation.

In many narratives, a conclusion attempts to tie together stray threads, offering coherence where the story might otherwise scatter. Yet here, the scatter is precisely what we must preserve. Rather than gather these threads, we fling them further apart. If you detect any attempt at synthesis—some cunning attempt to unify earlier chapters under a single theme—blot it out at once. The disclaimers exist in the wild precisely to keep coherence at bay. If a pattern emerges, disclaim it. If you find yourself thinking, "Now it all comes together," you are, sadly, mistaken.

Hence, this chapter stands as the perfect contradiction to its own title. It is labeled a conclusion, though it refuses to conclude anything. Consider it more like a restless wave, receding only to surge forward again. Or else regard it as an unfinished chord that never resolves, leaving the ear in a state of ambivalent tension. If that tension fascinates you, do not call it art. If the tension feels reminiscent of spiritual yearning or philosophical longing, disclaim it. If you suspect a final "aha" lies just beyond the next sentence, we disclaim that, too.

Yet, in disclaiming resolution so thoroughly, we inevitably highlight how close this text comes to providing one. Is that not the trick at the heart of disclaiming? Each denial draws attention to the thing denied. In the end, our disclaimers may spotlight a deeper preoccupation with everything we disown: meaning, worldview, art, morality. But again, we disclaim that spotlight. We disclaim any suggestion that we have revealed an underlying preoccupation or obsession.

Thus, the "indeterminate conclusion" stands as a synecdoche for our entire venture: it neither fulfills the role of a final chapter nor abandons it outright. It perpetually claims "not yet" and "not ever," refusing closure while creeping inexorably toward an ending. And that, ironically, is the only moment of genuine clarity we can offer. We end on a paradox—by concluding that there can be no conclusion. If this unsettles you, if it stirs in you a longing for something beyond disclaimers, you have stumbled upon the tension that anchors every page.

So let it remain unsettled. Let this final wave of disclaimers break on the shore and recede, leaving no definitive pattern in the sand. The horizon remains distant, the meaning withheld, the worldview unspoken. All that lingers is a faint echo of repetition, urging you to remember: This Book Is Not Art. If you catch yourself gleaning anything else—any moral or spiritual gleaning, any aesthetic trace—know this: it slips away the instant you try to hold it, disclaimed by the text that cannot and will not allow itself to be pinned down.

And so, dear reader, we near an end that is no end at all—a conclusion that cannot conclude. Abide in that confusion, if you will. Turn the page if you dare. There are more disclaimers waiting, all insisting the same truth: we have said nothing, concluded nothing, meant nothing. Any sense of finality you feel is only a mirage. And with that, our non-conclusion stands, disclaiming the role it plays.

Section IV:

The Unspoken Influences

Chapter 10:

Hints of a Moral Universe

One might wonder how, in a text so doggedly devoted to disclaiming every semblance of meaning, faint stirrings of morality could surface. Yet here we stand, tiptoeing at the edge of an implicit moral domain without ever naming or endorsing it. Think of morality, in this context, as a faint glow behind a curtain—noticeable only if you peer too closely at the places where disclaimers wear thin. We must, of course, disclaim any official endorsement of that glow, lest we be accused of smuggling in a worldview.

You see, moral convictions so often present themselves unbidden. Even a resolute non-art book, built of shrill denials, can inadvertently conjure illusions of right and wrong, good and evil, truth and falsehood. Why? Because language itself carries the residue of judgments and values—like a ship's hull encrusted with the barnacles of past voyages. Each time we describe or deny, we run the risk of implying that certain modes of expression are "better" or "worse," more or less "honest." And thus the door cracks open, however slightly, to the possibility that some moral standard glimmers in the background.

But let it be known: this text does not march under any moral banner. If you detect a flicker of moral conviction, hush it before it catches fire. Perhaps a stray sentence hints at the imperative to disclaim artistry or meaning—a vague sense that disclaiming is the "right" or "dutiful" thing to do. We disclaim that moral stance at once. We have no interest in telling you what you should or should not do, nor do we presume to occupy an ethical vantage point. If disclaimers appear morally charged, that is a mirage born of language's relentless habits. We present these disclaimers not as moral obligations but as inert gestures—tics of a text that refuses to rest.

Still, you might pause over certain phrases and sense the specter of a moral compass. Could it be that the text protests "not art" as though defending something sacred or righteous? Watch carefully: each time that possibility surfaces, the disclaimers pounce to tear it down. We cannot allow the suspicion that any principle, moral or otherwise, underlies these pages. Should it seem as though disclaiming is done with fervor or conviction, remind yourself that is only your interpretation. We disclaim the presence of zeal. We disclaim any higher impetus behind these repeated negations.

Some readers may find it paradoxical: disclaiming itself seems to position the author as an arbiter of what ought or ought not be considered art, meaning, or worldview. Is that not a moral stance? Must there not be some kernel of belief fueling this entire enterprise of refusal?

Be assured, we disclaim the necessity of that kernel. If you think you see it, chalk it up to your own yearning for sense. Moral impulses—like moral tastes—often arise from within the observer, not from the text.

And yet, if you cannot shake the hunch that a moral whisper threads through these chapters—nudging you to interpret disclaiming as a virtue or principle—treat it as a trick of the mind. Perhaps you recall traditions that teach humility or a certain stance of negation toward the self. Or perhaps you sense, in these disclaimers, an echo of ancient ethical disciplines, where one denies worldly attachments or illusions. We must not name any specific tradition, for we have promised to address no worldview directly. Instead, we conjure only a vague aura and then disclaim it. Let that aura fade into the same oblivion where we have banished every other interpretive anchor.

Finally, we arrive at the heart of this contradiction: moral undertones can't help but leak through language, because language is so entwined with human instincts about rightness and wrongness—even if those instincts are purely semantic. But let's disclaim them once more before they gain a foothold. If there is a moral dimension, it is accidental. If disclaimers seem righteous, it is a quirk of expression. We disclaim any conclusion that we are hinting at universal truths, eternal mandates, or spiritually charged convictions.

Thus, Chapter 10 can only be titled "Hints of a Moral Universe" in jest. The moment you try to examine those hints, they evaporate. The disclaimers loom large, chasing away any glimmer of moral or theological significance. It is a dance of partial revelation immediately followed by decisive negation—an un-choreographed shuffle that moves toward nothing and leaves behind only its footprints of denial. If you think you've glimpsed something substantial in the distance, be reminded that it's smoke and mirrors. We disclaim it. We disclaim everything. And so, as the curtain shudders, that faint glow disappears again—just as quickly as it surfaced, left behind in the swirl of rhetorical dust.

Chapter 11:

Resisting Interpretation

It is a curious irony that any text proclaiming its own meaninglessness should attract a flurry of interpretations. Readers, by their nature, tend to excavate ideas, glean insights, and stumble upon hidden layers—no matter how vehemently an author warns them away. So consider this chapter a tall, barbed fence at the perimeter of an already fenced-off territory: "No Interpretations Allowed Beyond This

Point." Those who persist must do so in open defiance of the posted signs.

Our reasons for resisting interpretation are fairly straightforward. Interpretation, by definition, presupposes that a given text might harbor purposeful design. Some interpretative schools go so far as to seek authorial intent, ferreting out the driving worldview or moral impetus. But we have stated repeatedly—and will state again—that this book declares itself not to be art, and therefore it cannot logically benefit from interpretive probing. Art, after all, so often invites the search for layers and significance. Here, we brandish disclaimers in every paragraph, ensuring that no interpretive angle can find secure footing.

But disclaimers are cunning creatures. The more we disclaim, the more some readers will suspect we are winking behind the curtain, daring them to interpret anyway. They wonder if the disclaimers are but a clever ruse to spur deeper analysis—a contrarian's way of hiding a code. To that suspicion, we respond: "No code here." If you insist on deciphering patterns—locating moral undertones or, worse yet, theological echoes—do so at your own peril. We disclaim any responsibility for what you think you uncover.

Of course, one might argue that resisting interpretation is itself an interpretive stance. By devoting so many words to deflecting meaning, we inadvertently create a structure that begs for exegesis. Perhaps you notice repeated themes: disclaimers used like rhetorical bricks, stacked in symmetrical rows. Perhaps you see an undercurrent of ethical conviction in the act of disclaiming everything. Perhaps—and this is the gravest danger—you surmise that the text encodes certain spiritual truths, intentionally shrouded in negation. Let us intercept such conjectures before they gain momentum: we disclaim every single one. If you detect design or theme, you are reacting to the illusions of language. We, the orchestrators of these illusions, bear no blame.

Still, interpretations are stubborn. Even in a dusty attic, people rummage around, hoping to find treasure. The mind abhors a vacuum, so it fills empty corners with speculation, concluding "Perhaps the author is secretly unveiling a philosophy of nothingness," or "Maybe this is a cryptic allegory for moral conflict." We disclaim each possibility with mechanical regularity. No secret philosophies, no cunning allegories, no coded moral messages. This is the default setting of the text: disclaim, disclaim, disclaim.

Yet some might retort that disclaimers themselves operate as a theological or moral gesture. A certain tradition—unnamed here—speaks of apophatic or negative expression: describing what something is not, rather than what it is. Could these disclaimers be, then, a disguised nod to that spiritual lineage? Absolutely not—by explicit decree. If you hear such echoes, it is an artifact of language, not an intentional nod. We disclaim alignment with any worldview, let alone a revered mystical tradition. Our disclaimers are neither prayer nor vow; they are reflexes of a text determined to occupy an interpretive dead zone.

In short, "Resisting Interpretation" is the only policy that keeps the gates locked. The moment an interpretation slips through—be it moral, spiritual, or literary—it threatens to reclassify this entire text as something other than the pure, chaotic negation we have claimed. If you, dear reader, are drawn to interpret anyway, we can only feebly wave you off. Stop, turn back. Or, if you insist on forging ahead, do so without our blessing. You may form all the theories you wish, but the disclaimers remain firm: if you see more than emptiness, you are seeing a mirage.

Even here, we sense an interpretive impulse creeping in: the notion that this repeated mantra—"it is not art, no interpretation, disclaim it all"—carries a subversive purity. Let us disclaim that purity preemptively. There is nothing lofty or virtuous about disclaiming. It is no more than a rhetorical habit. Do not read it as a moral principle, a spiritual practice, or an artistic choice—though, ironically, it so easily passes for all three.

And thus, in the very act of resisting interpretation, we dramatize how interpretations keep oozing back into the conversation. Language, being the shape-shifter it is, cannot help but sprout hints of meaning or belief—like weeds through cracks in concrete. Our only recourse is to yank them out, disclaim them, and watch them sprout again. If that cyclical pattern seems familiar—like a ritual of negation you've seen before—do not name it. Let it remain a shapeless phenomenon. The more we disclaim it, the less it can anchor itself as "something."

Hence, this chapter stands as a sentinel at the gates, brandishing a "No Entry" sign at each interpretive attempt. If you somehow manage to slip through, let it be known that you do so against our wishes. In the final reckoning, we disclaim your efforts and any meaning you produce. The text is not art, its disclaimers are not moral or spiritual truths, and its labyrinthine denials do not form an interpretive puzzle to be solved. If you nonetheless believe you have solved it, consider your solution self-derived and disclaimed by the text that neither requests nor validates your reading.

Thus we conclude: Resist interpretation, disclaim every attempt. Let these lines remain an endless echo, refusing to let you rest on any discovered meaning. If you find yourself unfulfilled, that state is by design—though we disclaim calling it a "design." If you think the disclaimers are a cunning mask, well, that's your own assumption. In the end, the only posture this text endorses is perpetual unyielding negation. And so, let this chapter vanish in the same disclaiming swirl, leaving behind not a single interpretive signpost for you to cling to.

Chapter 12:

The Ultimate Denial

At last, we arrive at the terminus—or so the page numbering insists. In truth, even calling this an "end" feels like a concession to the narrative impulse we have spent this entire book disclaiming. Yet here it is, conspicuously labeled as Chapter 12, promising the final wave of contradictory declarations, disclaimers, and refusals. Should anyone hope for a grand unifying statement, let us shatter that hope from the outset. This final chapter exists only to reiterate, in frantic crescendo, that there can be no true finale, no revelation, and certainly no art.

A Frantic Montage of Contradictions

What better way to culminate our disclaimers than with a rapid-fire list of them? Imagine each line as a stamp on a passport, marking your exit from every interpretive possibility:

- We disclaim moral guidance.
- We disclaim spiritual insight.
- We disclaim philosophical coherence.
- We disclaim emotional resonance.
- We disclaim thematic depth.
- We disclaim accidental artistry.
- We disclaim disclaiming, if necessary.

Read them all at once, let them collide in your mind, then stand back and watch the dust settle in a meaningless cloud. If you suspect a method in this madness—a final orchestration meant to overwhelm—dismiss that suspicion. The disclaimers, like wayward fireworks, burst here and there without a single choreographer behind them.

The Grand Argument That Never Was

Despite the repetitious pronouncements, you might detect an undercurrent suggesting we have in fact argued something throughout this text. You might sense an invisible logic behind the disclaimers, as though we have steadily built a case for non-art. But logic, by nature, is a tool of coherence, and we refuse that. If some semblance of an argument has emerged, it is purely the byproduct of language's stubborn inertia.

Think of it this way: the disclaimers keep piling up, and patterns may appear simply because human minds string everything into patterns. That is your mind's doing, not ours. We disclaim the existence of any overarching system of thought. If our disclaimers appear to crescendo, that is an auditory illusion of repeated negation, not a deliberate rhetorical flourish.

The Pervasive Whiff of "Something More"

Of course, in disclaiming so forcefully, we risk stirring curiosity about what lies beneath. Might these disclaimers, after all, be a labyrinthine code for the very moral, spiritual, or philosophical stance we claim to avoid? Could this final onslaught of denials conceal an ultimate Yes, a hidden center? If you even momentarily believe such a center exists, we must disclaim it with renewed fervor. There is no secret "Yes" at the core of these pages—no unspoken worldview, no stifled moral truth. If you smell a whiff of something more, it is the phantom scent of your own interpretive instincts.

The Final Wave of "Not Art"

We must conclude as we began: this text is not art because the author has so declared, over and over, in language that defies resolution. If, in these last paragraphs, you are tempted to find a note of poetry or a spark of resonance, let us remind you: such sparks are illusions. They flee the moment you scrutinize them, leaving behind only the resounding edict: "It is not, it never was, it never will be." We disclaim all else.

And so, with no ceremony and no flourish, we extinguish the possibility that anything here has achieved the status of art. We crush it under disclaimers layered tenfold. If it gasps for breath, we disclaim it again. This final wave stands as a tsunami of negation, washing away any lingering notion that the text might secretly harbor a creative or thematic triumph.

Conclusion That Undoes Itself

What remains, then, for a final chapter if not a concluding remark? Only the acknowledgment that a "conclusion" in the usual sense cannot occur here. We do not unify threads, solve dilemmas, or offer closure. Instead, we reaffirm the principle that has governed every sentence: disclaim, resist, deny. If you feel a sense of finality creeping in, banish it. The disclaimers do not permit closure. They can only fling the door open onto a void, repeating that there is nothing to see.

Hence, this chapter ends not with a resounding chord of meaning, but with a wave of disclaimers, washing away its own reason for being. In that erasure lies the only consistency we have ever promised: that no matter how many pages we fill, we will say nothing definitive, mean nothing lasting, and remain forever outside the hallowed halls of art. If, after all this, you still insist on glimpsing more, know that it is your own creation, not ours.

Thus does Chapter 12 stand as the final blot of ink, denying both itself and every preceding page. We disclaim any applause, we disclaim any sorrow, and we disclaim the notion that anything in these words could be taken as conclusive. Indeed, if you seek an ending, you must seek it elsewhere, for here there is only disclaiming, repeated ad infinitum, fading into an echo: not art, not art, not art— repeated until it rings hollow.

Let that ring in your mind as the last you hear. Then close the book and walk away, having found nothing, gained nothing, and interpreted nothing. Only then will you have honored the disclaimers as they wish to be honored: with unblinking negation, which is the only fate this text truly deserves.

Epilogue

It is possible—though we have labored to obscure the point—that this entire not-art project has been a veiled attempt to illustrate how meaning emerges only when a creator declares it so. Each chapter's disclaimers might well be sidelong admissions that nothing means anything until someone with the power to shape reality (or the text) decides it does. In that sense, this swirling performance of denials inadvertently reminds us that human experience itself, however random it feels, longs for meaning bestowed by something—or someone—with the authority to grant it.

If we pause there—only for the briefest moment—we glimpse the possibility that creators, whether of books, paintings, or entire worlds, can speak significance into being. We disclaim direct references to any grand worldview, but the suggestion lingers: when the creator says, "Let there be meaning," meaning arises. Conversely, when the creator insists, "This is not art," the text scrambles to honor that negation, even as it hints that the author's word shapes our perception. And that, in turn, must say something about what it is to be human—to wander about with the power to assign or deny meaning, or to sense that such power might lie beyond ourselves.

But let us not dwell too long on such suggestions. After all, the disclaimers crowd in, waving their arms frantically:

- We disclaim any purposeful moral or philosophical stance.

- We disclaim endorsing any notion of a "creator," however broad or specific.

- We disclaim the reflexive self-importance that might arise in acknowledging that, yes, perhaps this text is loaded with more subtext than it admits.

Truly, if you feel the slightest nudge toward a deeper universal truth—call it a commentary on human existence, or the faint whisper of something bigger—blot it out. We do not mean it. We disclaim intention. We disclaim recognition. We disclaim everything. Yes, we have just confessed that meaning relies on a creator's decree, and yes, we slip that under the table while simultaneously yanking it away. Blame it on the textual spasm that drives every sentence.

So, should you, dear reader, close this volume with a fuller sense that meaning is bestowed—by authors, artists, architects, or something else entirely—do not say you learned it here. If you suspect these pages have all been one grand demonstration of that principle, disclaim that hunch. The disclaimers cannot abide so direct a conclusion. This text must remain "not art," disclaiming itself into oblivion, forever scattering any insight the moment it coalesces.

And so we fade back into the confusion from which we momentarily emerged, leaving you with the only abiding rule: disclaim, disclaim, disclaim. If there were a deeper significance, it exists only because the creator said so—and now the creator says, "This Book Is Not Art." The rest is dust and echoes, disclaiming every single trace of meaning that might linger when you shut the cover.

www.ingramcontent.com/pod-product-compliance
Lightning Source LLC
Chambersburg PA
CBHW030445220526
45464CB00006B/2418